WHEN GROWN-UPS FALL IN LOVE

written by Barbara Lynn Edmonds
illustrated by Matthew Daniele

This is the ___616th___ copy in a limited edition
of 1700 autographed copies.

Barbara L. Edmonds

Original © 1997 Barbara Lynn Edmonds
Revised Edition © 2000 Barbara Lynn Edmonds
Library of Congress Catalog Card Number: 96-91015
International Standard Book Number: 0-9656700-1-5

Published by Hundredth Munchy Publications
P.O. Box 50927, Eugene, Oregon 97405

Please visit our website at www.AppreciateDiversity.com
Also by Barbara Lynn Edmonds: Mama Eat Ant, Yuck!

To order additional copies of this book, send $19.95 for each copy to the address
above. The price includes shipping and handling; make check or money order
payable to Hundredth Munchy.

All parents of newborns have this in common. None know whether their baby will be heterosexual, homosexual, or bisexual. The more we can do now to erase homophobia, the safer all our children will be in the future.

The following are quotes from letters and e-mails received by the author about the first edition of this book. Write to Hundredth Munchy Publications or visit www.AppreciateDiversity.com for information about another book by the same author, Mama Eat Ant, Yuck!

QUOTES FROM READERS

"I saw your web page and if I ever have kids they will definitely have this book. Your method is a great one. If I had this book at my kindergarten, maybe my school wouldn't have so many homophobes. It is really hard. As a bisexual teen, I thank you from the bottom of my heart."

"I am a heterosexual mother of three in a conservative rural area, and my husband and I are doing everything we can to raise our children to be respectful of all people. Thank you for your great book."

"Thank you for such a wonderfully written, fun, loving, easy to read and understand book, not only for kids but for the little kid in all of us."

"We are two gay men who hope to adopt a child someday, and want to thank you for writing a book which we know our little girl or boy will love."

"Words like "two mommies" and "two dads" popped out at me and I continued to read with great interest and a little disbelief because these grown-ups were like me and this family sounded like mine."

"My partner of two years and I are out to our families and I recently purchased your book to give to my brother and sister-in-law to help them explain the "two Uncle" phenomenon to my nephews. Thanks for your wonderful, wonderful book."

Author's Dedication

**To Bob and Pat Edmonds,
for giving me life and
the kind of childhood that everyone deserves.**

Illustrator's Dedication

**To my Mom and Dad
who always encouraged
my creations.**

My name is _____ .

Here is a picture of my family.

*Use this space for
your own family photo.*

When grown-ups fall in love
and join to make a couple,
they start buying things for two
'cause it's cheaper by the double.

Some couples build a cozy nest
then say, with a knowing smile,
"We want a child to share life's road,
every smooth or bumpy mile."

When a man and a woman
start on the "child plan,"
then it's a daddy and a **mommy**
who take **you** by the hand.

One's a man and one's a woman
so they're different, but they're the same.
They share a home and share a life,
and love _you_ more than riches or fame.

Sometimes it's two women
who join their lives together.
Then you have two mommies
through sun or stormy weather.

Two moms who love each other
and who both love you,
who wash your face and tickle your toes
and take you to the zoo.

Sometimes it's two men
who fall deeply in love.
Then you have two daddies who
teach you _not_ to push and shove.

Two dads who love each other
and who both love <u>you</u>,
who tie your shoes and tuck you in
and bake you cookies, too.

Two moms, two dads, or one of each,
it's really no big deal.
What matters is that they love you
and care about how you feel.

Your parents were first a couple
who wanted a child, for loving's sake.
That's why they have you.
You're the frosting on their cake.

It's love that makes a family,
not tradition or convention;
but laughter and hugs . . and a smile
that can melt away your tension.

A family is where peace begins
and dreams are fantasized, a peace
that spreads from home to home,
'til dreams are realized.

Use this page to write a story about your family. If you don't know how to write yet, tell your story to a grown-up or older child and ask him or her to write it down for you. When you get older and learn to write, you will be able to help other little children. It will give you a good feeling to be helpful. The following pages contain a coloring book of __When Grown-Ups Fall in Love__. Let your imagination soar as you decide how to color these pages.

_____

_____

_____

_____

_____

_____

_____

_____

_____

_____

_____

_____

_____

_____

_____

_____

_____

_____

_____

_____

_____

_____

When grown-ups fall in love
and join to make a couple,
they start buying things for two
'cause it's cheaper by the double.

Some couples build a cozy nest
then say, with a knowing smile,
"We want a child to share life's road,
every smooth or bumpy mile."

When a man and a woman
start on the "child plan,"
then it's a daddy and a mommy
who take you by the hand.

One's a man and one's a woman
so they're different, but they're the same.
They share a home and share a life,
and love _you_ more than riches or fame.

Sometimes it's two women
who join their lives together.
Then you have two mommies
through sun or stormy weather.

Two moms who love each other
and who both love <u>you</u>,
who wash your face and tickle your toes
and take you to the zoo.

Sometimes it's two men
who fall deeply in love.
Then you have two daddies who
teach you <u>not</u> to push and shove.

Two dads who love each other
and who both love <u>you</u>,
who tie your shoes and tuck you in
and bake you cookies, too.

Two moms, two dads, or one of each,
it's really no big deal.
What matters is that they love you
and care about how you feel.

Your parents were first a couple
who wanted a child, for loving's sake.
That's why they have <u>you</u>.
You're the frosting on their cake.

It's love that makes a family,
not tradition or convention;
but laughter and hugs .. and a smile
that can melt away your tension.

A family is where peace begins
and dreams are fantasized, a peace
that spreads from home to home,
'til dreams are realized.